ISBN: 978-1-7347655-3-3

Cover Design by Shelby Rashap
Book Design by G.C. Saiz

First Edition 2020

Pale Rose Publishing
pale.rose.publishing@gmail.com

CHAPTER ONE

Dedication

To everyone who believes in me and my dreams, especially my mother.

CHAPTER TWO

Keepers

They go hand in hand,
the keeper and the kept.
One loves, while the other thinks *once…*
once, all of this comfort quieted me.

The keeper and his pet,
she knows there can be more.
Once, all of this luxury subdued her,
back when wanting was the baseline.

She knows there should be more,
wants to be needed and not need.
Back when wanting was the baseline,
things were never *did*, but instead *done for*.

Not needful, but needed,

she grabs the mantle and pulls herself up.
Things get done, no *for* in sight.
There is plenty of strength in words.

She grabs the sword and plunges it down,
takes an eye and turns it around,
knowing there is strength in action.
They go hand in hand.

CHAPTER THREE

Poisonous Starlight

She wore night like it wasn't poison,
  as if a dream had never peeled her skin
off,
  or done something worse than kill her.
  As if she had never been betrayed by a
pretty face,
  or a comforting voice in a sunlit wood.

  I don't understand how anyone can sleep
through the night,
  and not wake up with their eyeballs
missing
  or a little slump to their shoulders.

  I'm sobbing into a girl's arms,
  and she is not understanding.

4

Everyday, the World Would End

She loved night like it was a sunrise,
as if the opportunity was the same
whether it was the sun who gave it,
or the moon,
as if stars were windows,
but the blackness was not a blind.

I could not understand her.
All of this poisonous starlight, infecting
me.
On the other hand,
on every other hand,
starlight, lifting her away.

CHAPTER FOUR

Fun, One Syllable

It's supposed to be fun,
   but most days I am so lost in the thickets,
   tearing brand new pants on thousand year
old thorns,
   that I can't tell if I'm being eaten by a lion,
   or cuddled by a koala.
   All I can think is,
   something is happening to me, and
   doesn't that mean something profound?

Honestly, I could do without the theatrics,
   because I know it could be fun,
   but all I can see are tail-up pennies,
   blaming them for everything wrong about
my day,
   and all I can do is pretend to everyone

Everyday, the World Would End

around me
    that, yes, I can tell a mountain
    from a molehill,
    and of course I know the definition of
unimportant,
    it's practically tattooed across my ass
    at this point,
    so let's stop asking questions.
    Isn't this supposed to be fun?

CHAPTER FIVE

What Is It With the Bees?

Let me know if I'm annoying you.
I mean, the world doesn't get to shatter
everyday
    so let me begin.
My voice doesn't toll, it rings incessantly,
not like a bee, buzzing with purpose,
but like a bell on the end
of a toddler's rattle.
Yet I happen to like the clarity
and obscenity of it,
thanks so much for noticing.

I mean, I don't get to stomp
on my own foot very often,
so why don't I put on some boots?

My ability to catch a football doesn't exist,
   but it pops up as a life test every now and
again,
   not like a bee sting,
   where the bee feels pain along with you, a
single event,
   but like a wasp attack,
   endless and terrible, everyone cheering on
   the wasp for whatever reason.

I happen to value brains more than
brawn,
   thank you very much,
   and you know, I love these debates,
   whatever they're about,
   but don't forget to let me know
   if I'm annoying you.

I mean,
I'd hate to.

CHAPTER SIX

Flamenco Words

I'm waiting for someone to ask me to
dance.
Not a jig, I don't want to make a fool of
myself,
but the sevillanas, something I know,
or at least used to.

I'm waiting for strong arms to start
to circle me and to pull back
just before I think I can hold them forever.

I'm waiting for passion to disguise itself
as delicate movements,
or as a story I've overlooked
dozens of times.
Maybe a man I've heard sung about,

but never heard sing.

I'm waiting to belong somewhere with
someone,
   not a single nail, but a whole toe,
   roaring thunder all around our own stage.

CHAPTER SEVEN

Depression, Trying to Get My Attention

I need help hurting you.
All these storm clouds do
is gray up the blackness I'm trying to
spread.
The rocks I throw through your windows
have the horrible habit of turning
into geodes.
More than a silver lining,
they seem like gifts don't they?

I wanted to hurt you,
steal the ends of your sentences
and make sure to leave them blank,
open for anyone to finish,
a fate worse than death,

but you always have words, don't you?

I forgive myself. I forgive myself. I forgive myself.

Will you shut up with the forgiveness?!
I would strangle you if I had arms,
but you've taken them from me.
I would stab you in the back,
but you've locked me in a room of
pillows.

Why won't you face me like a man?
Why won't you give me a weapon?
Are you afraid yet?
Are you sad?

Will you please stop saying
I forgive you?

CHAPTER EIGHT

It Always Matters

This is what happens
when you turn on yourself.
If I've told you once,
I've said it at least three times.
Blue becomes purple becomes midnight,
and we all know how poisonous
your secrets are in the dark.

For the love of God, light a candle!

Even a single match would make more
sense
   than just sitting there.
   This is what happens
   when you let yourself think.
   Thoughts become wolves become

monsters
    and they all look like you, don't they?
    Why am I not surprised?!
    Don't ruin your own past,
    do not equate awkward with evil.
    If I've told you once...
    You know what, it doesn't matter.

CHAPTER NINE

Dark Moments

It's time, run away.
All of these monsters swallow
like night swallows day.

My shoes fall apart
whenever I dare cross lines.
Keep me on the ground.

Scared and defenseless,
I think someone needs to stand
because I will not.

CHAPTER TEN

Battle of Wills, and Depression, the Winner

By the way, I'm here to kill you.
I didn't think to make it clear,
what with the way you're always
Threatening me.
Why do you get to darken my skies,
if I don't get to strike you down
with lightning every now and then?

I'm coming through the door to haunt
you,
    prepared to bathe in your blood,
    drink my fill of your tears,
    eat your hair like spaghetti.

By the way, I'm trying to terrify you.

Everyday, the World Would End

It's my turn to be the reason
you cross to the other side of the street,
the reason you can't get out of bed,
the reason you start to find gray hairs
when you look in the mirror.

When you look in the mirror,
when you look in the mirror,
can you see me?

Because I
can't see
you.

CHAPTER ELEVEN

You're Doing Fine Because You're Moving

I don't know where you're going,
   where you think all of these dark paths
lead to,
   but I'll tell you one thing.
   They are not paved in cobblestones.
   Think instead femurs and tibia, patellas,
   legs of those who walked,
   but never truly went.

I'll tell you something else,
   look at the trees,
   see how they
   Reach and reach, but never touch the
clouds?
   Those are the arms of the people

19

who started and broke down
halfway through.

I don't know what you'll give to be the
exception.
I don't know what will happen if you are.

All I know is you're moving.

◆

CHAPTER TWELVE

Throw Me a Shovel

Mom, I have to do something.
All of this stress is eating my insides,
I'm starting to capitulate.

All of these dreams,
useless in their in-accessibility,
quartering my mind
as a crowd laughs,
as the blood sprays.

Mom, I'm pretty sure I'm dying
and it's all my fault.

I say, I want to drop out of college.
You say, that might be a bad idea.
And then I'll go,

My life is not mine, it's everyone else's.
My dreams are not dreams, just wishes,
aren't they?
My future is not a *boom*,
it's a *whoosh* isn't it?
How dare you say I'm nothing
because I need to run from stress?
Why can't you see
I'm having trouble accepting
the inevitability of death.?

That's when you start, *I never said…*

Except I'm already in the spiral,
I'm already digging.
There is no stopping me now.

CHAPTER THIRTEEN

I Want, I Want, I Want

I wanted to be the president.
I wanted to be my mom.
I wanted to be my mom,
when I was mostly my dad.
I wanted to be a painter.
I wanted to be the kind of girl who could
be
    painted by a painter.
I wanted to be the paint,
the mess on someone's apron,
or the color on anyone's wall.
I wanted to be anything to anyone.
I wanted to be known for something,
but probably not for this.
I wanted to be right
for once,

The person who could laugh
instead of being laughed at.
Then I wanted to be a writer.
I wanted to be a killer of sorts,
an angel of doom,
an avenger of my little girl self,
but I wanted to be loved at the same time.
I wanted to be hurt so
I could feel justified.
I wanted to be dead,
to be forgotten, to be put away,
Like an old doll no one cares about
anymore.
But then I wanted to be alive,
and I was confused about wanting to be
alive,
so I cried a lot, hit walls.
I broke things,
and then I wanted to be a
mountain, or the sky,
or maybe an ant.
I wanted to be neutral,
not to not care,
but at the very least,
not to care about myself
and my mistakes.
I wanted to be aware that once,
I had been neutral.

Everyday, the World Would End

Once, nothing was about death,
and a day was just a day.
I wanted to be the kind of girl
who could live through a moment
and come out unscathed.

CHAPTER FOURTEEN

Not Feeling Like Myself

I am not afraid all the time,
and anyhow, without fear I
would be nothing but my best memories.
It's possible I wouldn't be worried,
but then I wouldn't be me.

Don't pretend you don't love
my repetition, the way I can swing
on the same word for hours,
or how I dehumanize myself when
I feel my worst.

The big are made of the little,
And the little
Are nothing but tears mixed with rain.

Everyday, the World Would End

Does anyone care when a bird cries
outside?
Of course not.
It just sounds like a song.

CHAPTER FIFTEEN

This is What Crying Alone is Like

I must have been close to dying,
remembering the day as if
it was not a blessing, but a monster
I used to know, used to believe in,
like the one who lived under my bed, or
in the closet, but mostly in my head,
the one I still call my enemy.

I must have been close
to falling apart,
The stars were blinking out.
I remember the sun was not a sun,
it was an eye,
and in it I was not enough,
within it, I was drowning in the endless
heat,

unable to cool down
or see what was chasing me.

I must have been running, because
as close as I was to seeing pain as a friend,
I could hear my legs below me,
sloshing through my own ocean,
breaking the ice as I came across it.
Yes, I think I was trying, I must have
been.

My shoulder was not turned.
My tears had not been wiped away.

CHAPTER SIXTEEN

Never Happening

I needed to be the president.
I needed to be my dad,
I needed to be my dad, but in those ways,
I was my mom.
I needed to be the joke,
not the object, but the subject,
and somehow I needed to be hilarious in
my cruelty.
I needed to be able to throw
verbal punches.
I needed to be the stain, not the shirt.
I needed people to think I was stronger
than anyone else, that if I wanted to,
and I did want,
I could let them know I was better.
I needed to be listened to,

like a king can say anything
and have it be true,
and I needed to believe
whatever I said.
I needed to run towards, not away,
always wanting to defend myself,
build myself up,
turn myself into the entire sentence.
I needed not to be quiet,
not to be the reason I'm walking on
eggshells
    just like everyone around me.

I needed to do some needing,
to turn my wanting into action,
to not be able to live without
whatever it is
I think I needed.

CHAPTER SEVENTEEN

Careening

The world is mine to walk
and die on.
I take no salt with the boulders
I eat for breakfast,
wearing them down to pebbles
and dust the more I move,
and I am always moving.

Let me count the cadence
of your journey,
running toward and away,
uphill and down.

Every direction matters
because you are the engine,
and I am the wheels, and

Everyday, the World Would End

there are no brakes.

CHAPTER EIGHTEEN

Waiting Rooms and Roots

While you're waiting, why don't you
    let each drop of rain soak through your
marrow
    like an idiot?
    Or stand in the shower
    and turn the steam into flames,
    the flames into hell?

The sky has no idea why you're staring at
it,
    and the ground
    doesn't understand why
    you've put roots down here,
    right in the middle of where you
    should not be.

Everyday, the World Would End

This is a reason you're sad,
a reason why you're turning into winter,
why all of your leaves are on the ground
and you can't remember a time when
Your branches looked green.

Get away from me with your
definitions and destruction.
You act like hell is above and below you,
ahead and behind.
The right word is inside.

Does that mean it's real?

Anyways, while you were waiting...

CHAPTER NINETEEN

Creating Silence

I don't know anymore if
the words I say have any meaning,
or if, when they fall
to land on the wrong notes,
like a five year old's fingers
clutter up keys,
they aren't anything but fuel for
thunderstorms,
lightning strikes,
starting fires in my own fields
and starving me out of
my own valley.
Why can't I find the way
through the forest my words
have grown to stop me?
I'd burn it down if I wasn't here,

Everyday, the World Would End

in the middle of a line,
being choked by a line,
swallowing a line.
I just want to spit it out,
but I don't know anymore
how to help the babble
as it bubbles its last breath
into the silence I've created.

CHAPTER TWENTY

Where is the Lesson?

The takeaway disappeared
as soon as I laughed,
as soon as my eyes crinkled
and the air got warm as mid-July.
I wish I'd kept it cool,
let you know how hard it would be
to penetrate my chest,
so frozen solid, your fist
would have shattered the moment you
tried.
    But you wouldn't try.
    My glare would remind you of a blunt
dagger
    aimed at your throat.
    The possibility of pain
    would scare you away.

Everyday, the World Would End

Instead, I chuckle,
and that's the best way to put it
because I hate that word.
I hate losing dignity
over the need to protect myself.
I hate feeling lost
when there is only one place to be,
between a hot and a cold place.

CHAPTER TWENTY-ONE

Apocalyptic Jam

And then I had to thrive.
The point wasn't to be the sun after night,
to be someone else's reason.
All I wanted was to eat cake.

The point wasn't to be night after a hard
day.
How many fingers are held up when you
are happy?
All I wanted was to eat.
Ask yourself this question: *how hungry are
you?*

I hold up one finger.
The threat of starvation is contained in
ones.

Know this for sure: *how close are you to
dying?*
What will you do for a jar of jam?

Starvation is contained in one moment of
failure.
I need you to know that taste isn't fickle,
it's best defined as what you would do for
a jar of jam.
Of all things to consider, there is cruelty.

Taste changes, but sometimes, it doesn't.
It's yet to be determined if you are the
same.
Of all things to consider, there is kindness,
but then you have to survive.

CHAPTER TWENTY-TWO

Monster Made of Hugs and Talons

I know the face of my monster.
Coming from the bruised sky as if
she was the fist that forced the sun down,
she hisses my name across the battlefield.

What is the battlefield?
I am the battlefield, cracked and
crumbled,
　　potted with blood that matches the colors
　　of my insides, not blue but pastel,
　　not dull but dimmed.

I find myself waiting for her to kill me.
　　I want her talons to rip out my throat
sometimes,
　　but she never does, and sometimes

Everyday, the World Would End

I am grateful.

I am just standing there, expecting a show
of her swooping down and feasting
on the scraps I've left out,
not for her, but certainly not for myself.
But maybe I am the show?

All the time, she's laughing, dancing
around,
    like my screaming is music,
    as if each tear that hits the ground
    is a drum beat,
    a string plucked.

I wish I could hug her,
because sometimes when I hug people
they say *stop suffocating me!*
That's why she's here, because
I don't want to hug her,
because it didn't matter, but
of course it does.
I am made of little moments.

The ground falls away when she goes,
taking me with her, and the
pools of blood seem so far away...
When she drops me, maybe I'll float.

CHAPTER TWENTY-THREE

Depression, Ordering His Soldiers Around

Leave the young ones.
The air around them reeks of thyme
and swallow-shit.
I don't need one willful memory
standing up and bringing down
all the ones I want to multiply.

Find me one who screams when the wind
does,
  not the other way around, or, at the very
least,
  make sure she's tried, but will not try
again.

When the air is warm and spiced,

that's when we will bring our winters,
lead them in with twine
and stake them with thick chains.
She'll never understand what hit her!

Why are the clouds raining ash?
Where did the present go?

I can hear her voice now,
the crack of porcelain breaking,
an ice cube shattering quietly.

Then, and imagine this,
we'll light a bonfire.
We'll use the remains of her to start it,
the scraped-out bones,
the unwashed hair,
the nails she let grow out, because
she wasn't going anywhere.

I can't wait to breathe in the flames,
can't wait to see her,
just breathing.
I can hardly
wait.

CHAPTER TWENTY-FOUR

The Edge of Bullying

I am standing at the edge of my beliefs.
You must understand, below me
there is dark stone, unyielding,
above me, the eye of the storm,
a door I must not enter or exit, spiraling
up and up,
but the wind will never take me back
down.
I'm waiting for a claw to grab my
sweatshirt
and drag my scream
through the floor.
See, above them there is only sky,
and below them the everyday heat of
summer.
Let me know when the principal

opens his door and herds them in.
I want to hear him say,
I am standing
at the edge
of my silence.

CHAPTER TWENTY-FIVE

Tea and Reasoning

You forget to move.
The time, it stains your teeth
like tea, deep and sweet at first,
then the marks stay forever.
Forget about the metaphor,
do something.
Your day is wasting away as if
it has not deserved to eat in months
and you have forgotten to mourn it.
What is wrong with you?
All of this personified avoidance,
dancing around the fact that you
Have been sitting for five hours.
Hair flying on a made-up breeze,
feet in ten inch heels,
(the ground, it's too plain)

and a cultivated voice.
How dare you forget
the reason you woke up
this morning?
How dare you not have a reason
at all?

CHAPTER TWENTY-SIX

Angry Moments Turn to Oceans

Intensity swallows me,
a wave over my head, heavy,
heavy like air when it's heated,
heated like I will not walk away
without the need for more water.

I want to strangle you.

Fire can give life and take it.
I can ruin my own life and
forget I ever had one.
What is a superpower?

A redness consumes me,
a cat scratch on raw flesh.
The moment, it's only a moment,

Everyday, the World Would End

and I will be here forever,
waiting for the waves to
take up the shore,
steal the air, and turn
my lungs to fire.

CHAPTER TWENTY-SEVEN

Yes, I Dare...

You're listening to music.
The beat drops.
Someone is in your house,
wishing you'd step to the left,
just a little bit.
Clear shot, and all that.
Hear me now, and what's more.
You step to the right.
Being contrary is a recessive gene,
or at least in your line it is.
Someone is surprised that
yes, you dared,
and they're making for the window,
because why can't you be an easy kill?
Just lie down and merge with the
doormat?

Everyday, the World Would End

The beat drops again.
Someone is outside.
You are in the kitchen,
head anywhere but in the oven.

CHAPTER TWENTY-EIGHT
Stability is a Golden Word

No I'm not.
This frustration is enough to kill me,
even if I can't hold the knife myself.
Let me go.
The sun has turned black,
the moon gray, but
the stars are still white,
still white because they are far away,
and the specks of my insides can't reach
them.
Don't you see? I've tried,
but am too weak to try again.
I play with knives in the kitchen,
imagining what would happen if I dared,
if only I dared.
Do I need to spell it out?

Writing out tables of possibility
has grown old. Sometimes,
I think I can begin.
Three by three equals a circle.
Go to jail. You are in a circle,
Three by four equals a square.
Four points out of a hundred...
Why not just...
Can't you just...
Three by five and magically I'm fine
again.
Three by six, *no I'm not.*

CHAPTER TWENTY-NINE

Writing a Poem in Comparison

Throw out a line and see
if it floats.
I'm not one for sunlight falling
through a window, landing perfectly
on a journal page, lighting the way.
I'm more a pile of dirt and lawn debris
when the vacuum is on the other side
of the house
and a gust of wind is coming
to blow me away
without anyone knowing.
You know what I mean?
All of these analogies and I'm
still waiting for the vacuum.
Where is the hook when I need it?
Where is the salmon?

Everyday, the World Would End

All I have are gently-gummed sardines,
and everyone hates them.
I've never been one for eating spaghetti
with a fork, I've always
preferred spoons, haven't you?
Someone throw me a line,
I'm floating.

CHAPTER THIRTY

Hating Myself to Sleep

Like the beginning of a song,
where all paths can lead to love or hate,
I breathe and then I scream,
never stopping through the night,
one note to live a life by.

Like my tongue is a snake,
or perhaps a shark, I must
keep going, writhing
and wasting energy, screaming,
because maybe if I'm loud enough,
someone will help me.

The way through is truly the stomach.
If you ever need to kill me,
shove a compliment down my throat

Everyday, the World Would End

and tell me to swallow.

Like a weed to a rose,
why bother?

Like setting an alarm,
what's the point?

Someone take the record off.
I'm going. Didn't you hear me?
I'm gone.

CHAPTER THIRTY-ONE

Sitting at Tables and Other Sinful Things

When I go beneath the ground,
to dance, *or perhaps to die,*
follow me and trace my path, and
pull me back, and
drag me back, and
join me at the table,
the table that is almost always a bed,
almost always the size of a salt sea,
almost always filled with dead-on-the-
inside fish
that love to watch me in particular.

When I wash up on some shore to sleep,
perhaps forever,
trace my path and bring me breakfast,

Everyday, the World Would End

and will you help me?
Will you wake me?
And won't you join me?
Together we'll feast on the stars
that died last night,
when we were underground,
at the table.

CHAPTER THIRTY-TWO

Fried Nerve Endings

Don't sweat it.
I'll be here counting the days
while you live them.
I may look sad, but
it's just my face
doing what it does,
after it doesn't feel a punch.
You know, nerve endings,
they stop working sometimes
in order to survive.
In other words, just give me
half a moment, and I'll
make a joke.
In other words, things will be normal,
and all of this snow,
it will melt, like the air

Everyday, the World Would End

is shedding a jacket
or protective armor,
like it's sweating.
Not that you need to sweat.
I didn't want to state the obvious,
but don't worry.
Sweat not.

CHAPTER THIRTY-THREE
And We Begged

And each line put on a show,
and every show was the last one,
and the last door closing meant
the first would open again,
and all of our clothing was red,
and whatever the apocalypse would be
it hadn't happened yet,
and all of this pain,
it was for something.
And there was an end,
and if there was a night,
there was also a horizon,
and the only true thing
was that a sun would rise again tomorrow
and no one would appreciate it,
because the sun rose everyday.

Everyday, the World Would End

And, one day, when it didn't,
and the sky turned dark, and the birds
didn't sing,
we stared at the stars and thought
this is enough.
And secretly, in the dead of day,
we screamed, and then we whispered,
and then we begged.
And it was never enough.

CHAPTER THIRTY-FOUR

But Then We Gave Up

But day had never been this dark before,
so dark, the wind had a color,
silver-white against the sky,
and the sun rising didn't matter
because sometimes, through the clouds,
we could see it,
and it was nothing but cold fire,
and we were afraid to leave our beds.
Sometimes, through the clouds,
we thought we could see Him,
and He was angry,
beating the clouds as if they might
fall and crush us,
but we were already crushed.
Our houses, they felt like jails, and
above and below meant the same fate.

Everyday, the World Would End

Everything that could be broken
mattered more than anything
and unbreakable things did not exist.
Give us a chance, we whispered,
but there was always a better answer,
and it had never been that dark before,
so dark, there was a future,
singular and solitary against the sky.

CHAPTER THIRTY-FIVE

Everyday, Long Ago

Can someone else go in and pay?
I'm tired of dead poplar leaves
crowning my head and helping me
through doors. I'm tired of praying
for less pain and more time.
Can someone just touch the handle,
pull a bit, and I swear I can pay,
all the mistakes you could ever want,
your face, seared on my brain,
my last words, I'll make them an apology,
just open the damn door,
because I can't, I cannot,
I will not open the door.
I no longer have enough to pay.

CHAPTER THIRTY-SIX

Everyday, in the Sky

Everyday, the world would end,
and the sun would say,
I will be back,
I am still here,
I would never leave,
but I could not believe the truth of my
own horizon,
that when night fell,
a new day was beginning for another,
that the mountains could not swallow,
only hide, and the ocean did not snuff,
only pause.

Everyday, the light would ebb,
and the moon would whisper.
Am I not proof?

Everyday, the World Would End

Am I not a sign?
Am I not enough?
But I could not be comforted by the truth
of my own heavens...

The stars were eyes,
dry and sobbing.
The moon was a mouth,
screaming and sighing.
And the sky, endless and moody,
was the nose,
breathing shallow.

Out and in.
Out, and then in.
Out...
Out...
Out, again...

CHAPTER THIRTY-SEVEN

Sleepless Creature

I'm looking into the wilds of my own
eyes.
    I'm lurking in the shadows they create,
the dark bags and wrinkled crevices
that say to the world,
this creature is cursed with realistic dreams,
with enemies within, but not without,
the harmful musings of someone who
pretends they are fine to their therapist
and only ever cries in front of their mother.

I am searching them for a light
that doesn't dim, for a dead look
of determination, but so far
    all I can tell is that they don't want to be
here,

Everyday, the World Would End

whatever it is that lives behind irises.

The bags are packed,
piled up in the cornea,
along with some leftover salt water.

At this point, I'm watching my own eyes,
praying for movement.

CHAPTER THIRTY-EIGHT

Dinner and Death, Death and Dinner

Her soul had thrown itself among
the dinner things.
Some of it was on the walls, blending
with the floral pattern as best it could,
but most was in the stew,
floating with the potatoes,
pretending to be bits of flotsam.

Indeed, her soul was drowning,
choking on salt and oregano,
but quite enjoying the process of death,
of burying itself in food.

As they sunk beneath the surface,
the pieces were smiling with their little
soul smiles,

they were inhaling
with their sniffing soul noses,
to help themselves along,
because it felt amazing.
This suffocation, it was great.
It's so much easier to sit than to stand,
to drown than to swim,
to fall, to take,
to eat,
than to resist.

What was left of her soul had hidden itself
within the pantry,
waiting for the door to open,
for the dinner things
to respectably be taken out.

CHAPTER THIRTY-NINE

The Past is a Bear Trap

The moments were crying.
Each one had the ability to be terrible,
to be the force behind the driver,
but they chose
to step into the bear trap that was the past
and let themselves bleed instead.

They weren't asking for help,
though many used that word
to lure well-wishers to them no doubt,
to make certain people knew
they (did) did not want to be there,
bleeding (bleating) out uselessly.

No, they did not enjoy lurking in the past.
Of course they were trying to forget.

The well-wishers turned to questioners,
and they passed the past by,
and the moments trapped there could
hear them
    asking one another,

    Why then?
    Why then?
    Why, then?

CHAPTER FORTY

Stability II

I felt like writing a song.
I thought, maybe, with my tongue falling out
from between my teeth
in a first grader's smile,
with my hair loose and wild, like I used to be,
perhaps it wouldn't sound so strained
when I sang *this is my life*
and my life is good,
and, just maybe, when I try to be happy,
people fall for it, and stop the refrain of
Are you sure? Are you sure?
With music and love in their voices.

It's like a song.

Everyday, the World Would End

Are you sure?
Are you sure?
Sweetie, let me know,
are you sure?

That would be the chorus, sung by angels,
and at last my voice would cut in,
quiet, then quieter, then even more so.

No I'm not,
no, I'm not.
Can't you see me?
No I'm not.

CHAPTER FORTY-ONE

Death's Account

Is this how I want it to end?
Around me, green seeps to brown,
life ebbs away as I move closer,
and I fear the asking has ended.
Now I must simply take.
People pretend they gave me permission,
or perhaps dropped a dance card
at my door, instead of me,
knocking on their's.

I'm sorry ladies, my night is full.
I cannot step away from the doors
I promised to guard,
or the prisoners I must take back
To wherever I came from.
My counterpart would not be happy,

and, really, neither would you.

Is this how you want to go?
Fighting me, not taking my hand,
but forcing me to pull you?
The door has closed. The light is out.

And you? You ask me. *You enjoy this?*
And I'd answer,
I have never been taught to fight,
with sword or stick or even words.
The only thing they tell you
on your first day is that
you have to win,
and so I do.

CHAPTER FORTY-TWO

Near the End, Ambiguous

Here's the plan…
See, there used to be these dreams,
and perhaps the best word
to describe them was *random*
because none of them had
a path, a body, or an ignition.

In fact, the only thing they had
was the will to exist,
the passion to take a single step,
or perhaps only half,
maybe a third,
and what they needed was a plan,
though no one wanted to mention it.

So here it is…

Everyday, the World Would End

You know, it's hard being the person
with ideas, when my arms
can't do a pull up and my eyes
can only see gold, not cry it,
and I'm not trying to make excuses,
but if there was a plan,
and there is, I swear,
I'd want everything to be perfect
before I started.

Maybe that's not a good idea, but listen...

If you want to hear the plan,
swing by tomorrow.

CHAPTER FORTY-THREE

Inspiration Scenting the Air and Running

I ran with a spiked club
and no destination,
a dangerous combination for
any hunter or writer.
The mountains were jagged.
The wind, cold as black ice.
And the fog was dense and
flavorless like peasant bread.

The air was not sweet,
the sun had not shone,
yet the scat was dry.

I swear, in the mountain pass,
someone was singing of heroes

Everyday, the World Would End

and death,
and along with the club on my back,
there was a drum,
and I wanted to join, wanted to kill,
whoever was singing,
to add percussion to what before
Was only humming,
to add words to their random sounds.

Inspiration is hard to follow,
leaving no footprints,
only deep scarring, as thinking tends to
do.